Tactical Air C
1946-9
Cold War Air Power

KEVIN WRIGHT

Front cover image: A Tactical Air Command (TAC) 'Wild Weasel' F-4G from the 37th TFW at George Air Force Base (AFB), departs on a Suppression of Enemy Air Defense training mission during 1988. (Fred Jones)

Title page image: A 363rd Tactical Reconnaissance Wing (TRW) RF-4C Phantom during a 1980 training mission. (USAF/TSgt Frank Garzelnick)

Contents page image: A sobering image of F-15s and F-16s above the burning Kuwaiti oil fields shortly after the end of Operation *Desert Storm* in February 1991. (USAF)

Back cover image: An 87th Fighter Interceptor Squadron (FIS) F-106A flies from its alert facility at Charleston AFB, South Carolina. In 1979, TAC had gained responsibility for the interceptor and ground radar elements of continental US air defenses. (USAF/TSgt Ken Hammond)

Published by Key Books
An imprint of Key Publishing Ltd
PO Box 100
Stamford
Lincs PE9 1XQ

www.keypublishing.com

The right of Kevin Wright to be identified as the author of this book has been asserted in accordance with the Copyright, Designs and Patents Act 1988 Sections 77 and 78.

Copyright © Kevin Wright, 2023

ISBN 978 1 80282 673 9

All rights reserved. Reproduction in whole or in part in any form whatsoever or by any means is strictly prohibited without the prior permission of the Publisher.

Typeset by SJmagic DESIGN SERVICES, India.

Contents

Chapter 1	Constant Flux	4
Chapter 2	South East Asia, 1964–72	11
Chapter 3	Back to the Cold War	17
Chapter 4	The Creech Years	24
Chapter 5	COBs and Coronets	28
Chapter 6	TAC Looks to the Middle East	46
Chapter 7	TAC Goes to War in the Gulf	52
Chapter 8	From TAC to Air Combat Command	91

Chapter 1
Constant Flux

Tactical Air Command (TAC) was formed on March 21, 1946, alongside Strategic Air Command (SAC) and Air Defense Command. Headquartered at Langley Air Force Base (AFB), it was responsible for operating at locations across the entire United States. Its units were tasked to conduct military operations outside the continental US, and its fortunes, like that of other major commands, fluctuated over the years. Experiencing near constant organisational changes, it remained at the forefront of United States Air Force (USAF) combat operations for the duration of the Cold War. TAC had a distinguished operational history, including action in Korea, South East Asia and the 1990–91 Gulf War, until it was transformed into Air Combat Command (ACC) on June 1, 1992. Its historical development was a complex one, as the aircraft it operated and the tasks it was required to perform were in a constant state of flux. In addition to its core task of mounting fighter and attack operations, TAC units sometimes included transport, air refueling and special forces elements.

While much smaller in personnel terms than Strategic Air Command, TAC operated many more aircraft. Its early composition was mainly of World War Two types, including P-47s, P-51s and the new P-80 Shooting Star. It took on close air support (CAS) tasks, interdiction and tactical reconnaissance and provided troop carrier support for US Army airborne forces. In 1948, TAC was assigned to serve under Continental Air Command (CONAC), which had been created to better manage Reserve and National Guard forces. Following the outbreak of the Korean War in 1950, it quickly became clear that CONAC was poorly suited to co-ordinating wartime operations, especially after TAC gained additional responsibilities

TAC returned the F-51 Mustang to service in the Korean War. Armed with rocket and bombs, the aircraft were frequently assigned ground-attack tasks. (NARA)

for tactical/forward air control, electronic warfare and some special operations forces. As a result, it was returned to a 'major command' status, directly reporting to HQ USAF as of December 1, 1950.

TAC faced numerous early challenges. In particular, its new single-engine jet aircraft, like the P-80 and F-86, were in short supply and lacked the range and loiter time often needed to provide good close-air support. In contrast, the older World War Two types, such as the F-51 Mustang, did have the range and loiter capability, but there were difficulties locating serviceable airframes and shortages of spare parts.

As the US war effort in Korea rapidly expanded, so did TAC's role. The immediate airlift of personnel and equipment to the US West Coast for onward movement to Korea and Japan stretched TAC resources. During this period, TAC transferred most of its B-45 fleet to SAC and Air Training Command. It simultaneously greatly expanded its B-26 bomber crew-training program, preparing them for World War Two-style tactical operations in Korea.

The F-86 Sabre aircraft was rapidly introduced to service and deployed to the Far East theatre. In September 1950, an Air Ground Operations School was formed at Pope AFB, to train Air Liaison Officers and Forward Air Controllers (FAC). Jump training for FACs commenced in January 1950, and

Right: The F-86 performed well in Korea, but even with extra fuel tanks it sometimes struggled with longer-range missions. (NMUSAF)

Below: The B-26 Invader was another World War Two aircraft returned to service in large numbers during the Korean War, including this specialist version fitted with early infrared sensors for night bombing. (NMUSAF)

TAC formally established an Electronic Countermeasures (ECM) office with a linked training program. At the beginning of 1951, TAC's inventory comprized 854 aircraft made up of C-45, C-46, C-47, C-82, C-119, B-26, B-29, B-45, F-51, F-80, F-82, F-84, F-86, RF-80, RB-26, RF-51 types, with assorted trainers and liaison aircraft and more than 21,000 personnel. By January 1952, it had mushroomed to 61,494 personnel with an aircraft inventory of 1,347, which included the newly introduced F-94 Starfire all-weather fighter and the ultimately unsuccessful C-122 twin-engined medium transport aircraft.

Above: Early versions of the F-84 Thunderjet suffered from a largely lacklustre fighter performance and were more successfully used in ground-attack roles. (NARA)

Left: Never living up to its 'all-weather interceptor' description, the F-94A/B Starfire served in Korea in small numbers and later some Air National Guard (ANG) units. (NARA)

In those early years, TAC was often overshadowed by the perceived glamour of Strategic Air Command, with its huge bombers and arsenal of destructive nuclear weapons. As a result, TAC was lower down the budgetary priority list. Senior US Air Force commanders recognized the need for TAC to forge a nuclear role of its own, to secure a future for tactical airpower and avoid it being completely sidelined. Until the Vietnam War, TAC prioritized its own 'sub-strategic' nuclear capability to deliver nuclear weapons over shorter distances than SAC's intercontinental capabilities. TAC contingency operations were expected to require transatlantic aircraft deployments to Europe, or elsewhere in the world, to counter any immediate crises. Given the large distances involved, these would nearly always require air-refueling support, generating a considerable requirement for aerial tankers alone. TAC's conventional tasks, particularly providing close air support to the Army, were moved down the list of its priorities.

TAC possessed its own airlift resources and later, for a brief period, added an air-refueling tanker capability of its own. TAC airlifters joined the Berlin Airlift in 1948 when its C-47s and C-54s were sent to Europe to assist United States Air Forces in Europe's (USAFE's) massive supply effort into the city. Similarly, transport operations during the Korean War were extensive, when in addition to its tactical supply and airdrop operations, TAC transport aircraft were employed for frontline airdrops and routine logistic flights between Japan and Korea, supporting the efforts of the Military Air Transport Service.

Strategic Air Command was the primary operator of the USAF's air-refueling force. As it began to receive its new all-jet KC-135A Stratotankers, SAC's retired KB-29M/Ps and KB-50Js were passed to Tactical Air Command. They were flown by six Air Refuelling Squadrons from July 1953 until the last was inactivated in February 1965.

TAC used bases in Japan to supply its forward airfields in South Korea and make frontline air drops. (NMUSAF)

TAC operated transport aircraft, like these C-119s, to air drop paratroopers and supplies during the Korean War. (NARA)

Passed to TAC from Strategic Air Command (SAC), a 420th ARS KB-50J, a derivative of the wartime B-29 bomber, modified as an aerial tanker. (RAF Sculthorpe Heritage Centre)

The KB-50Js were fitted with a probe and drogue refueling system, which was succeeded by the refueling boom equipment on the KC-135A, allowing for much more rapid fuel transfers. (RAF Sculthorpe Heritage Centre)

By 1956, TAC's inventory of 1,690 aircraft was a mix of F-84s, F-86s, F-100s, RF-80s, RF-84Fs, C-124s, C-119s, C-47s, B-26s, B-57s and KB-29s. They were spread between six troop carriers, four fighter-bomber, two day-fighter, one tactical reconnaissance and two bombardment wings, together operated by nearly 58,000 personnel. 1956 was a big year for TAC, with the arrival of new equipment. In January, the 513th Troop Carrier Group received its first C-123 Providers, followed by the 16th Tactical Reconnaissance Squadron and 363rd Tactical Reconnaissance Group (TRG), as the first TAC units to receive the Douglas RB-66C. In March, the 17th Bomb Wing (BW) converted to the B-66, and Langley AFB received its first KB-50 tankers in July. The following month, the first F-100Cs, with their in-flight refuelling capability, arrived. The first F-100Ds joined the 405th Fighter Bomber Wing (FBW) at Langley AFB in September, and on December 9, 1956, TAC's first C-130As became operational with the 463d Troop Carrier Wing, at Ardmore AFB, Oklahoma, to round off the year.

TAC's early years were characterized by frequent organisational changes, which often initially appeared random, including numerous wing and squadron activations and deactivations, accompanied by role changes. In context, those ten years also saw a huge equipment transition, moving from an all-propeller, subsonic force to a mainly jet, mostly nuclear-capable and supersonic fighter force. Similarly, there were other major tactical capability improvements that were enabled by the adoption of air refueling, improved night-attack capabilities and better tactics and training. Given the profound nature of some of these technical advances, it is hardly surprising that the organisational aspects continually struggled to keep pace.

One of those advances was TAC's development of its Composite Air Strike Force (CASF) concept, which had completed trials by 1956. This revolved around being able to "rapidly assemble and deploy a tailored force package comprising tactical fighter, bomber, reconnaissance, and support aircraft together with the personnel and equipment needed to sustain them in the field for periods up to 30 days." Preparing for CASF operations was described by TAC commander Gen OP Weyland as requiring it to assemble "suitable aircraft and equipment, planning, training, in-flight refuelling and fly-away kits," accompanied by the necessary training.

CASF's first real test was in July 1958 when a deployment was ordered to the Middle East to support the fragile Lebanese government, headed by President Camille Chamoun. The initial CASF deployment was far from flawless. "Of the first 12 airplanes [F-100s] to launch, one crashed en route, seven aborted into alternate fields along the flight path, and only four made it to Adana, Turkey." Five days elapsed before the full aircraft complement arrived at its destination. While this was far from inspiring, TAC refined its quick reaction capability over the following years. It soon enabled TAC to rapidly deploy and operate aircraft anywhere across the world, a capability that later became the cornerstone of its operational success.

By the time of the Cuban Missile Crisis in October 1962, TAC's frontline consisted of a nuclear-capable strike force, built around large numbers of F-100 Super Sabres and F-105 Thunderchiefs. When the crisis erupted, TAC rapidly moved aircraft to bases in the southeastern United States, increasing its presence from around 140 fighters to approximately 623 aircraft, including 511 fighter-bombers (F-100s and F-105s), 72 reconnaissance aircraft (RF-101s and RB-66s) and 40 tankers (KB-50s). When the crisis eased, these aircraft dispersed back to their regular bases, but soon a much bigger and longer-lasting task emerged for TAC.

RB-66Bs of the 363rd Tactical Reconnaissance Wing were forward deployed to the southeastern US during the Cuban Missile Crisis. (NMUSAF)

Chapter 2
South East Asia, 1964–72

Events beginning to unfold in South East Asia demonstrated the shortcomings of TAC's now primarily nuclear-strike role-orientated force. As the war in Vietnam ratcheted up from early 1965, the USAF and TAC presence rapidly expanded mainly operating from bases in Thailand and South Vietnam. For those early operations, aircraft and personnel undertook gradually lengthening periods of Temporary Duty (TDY), assigned to USAF Pacific Air Forces (PACAF) 7th and 13th Air Forces that managed in-theatre operations. Back in the US, the Air Force's and Tactical Air Command's training capacity was substantially increased as the war progressed and more resources were committed to it. This peaked in 1968, with more than 94,000 USAF personnel operating in Thailand and South Vietnam alone. Most were from TAC units, but that number included around 18,000 Air National Guard

TAC F-104Cs were briefly used in Vietnam between 1965 and 1966, mainly to fly combat air patrols protecting EC-121 Constellation airborne early warning (AEW) and electronic reconnaissance aircraft. This line of 479th Tactical Fighter Wing (TFW) F-104Cs is at Udorn Royal Thai AFB in1965. (USAF)

members and Air Force Reservists, with 1,760 aircraft spread between 85 squadrons. They represented 10 percent of the USAF's total strength at the time. TAC aircraft were mainly involved in ground attack missions, providing escorts to strike packages and SAC B-52 operations. Soon, flights of four, usually F-105 Thunderchiefs, went ahead of the main strike package to suppress enemy air defenses. For this highly dangerous 'Wild Weasel' mission, they were equipped to detect enemy surface to air missile and air defense radars emissions, which they subsequently attacked.

Flying over sprawling rice fields and above the dense canopies of the Vietnamese, Cambodian and Laotian jungles, TAC was called upon to perform countless close air support (CAS) missions for US, South Vietnamese and friendly troops. It also hit enemy supply lines and troop concentrations. TAC soon

Above: F-100Ds were widely used in close air support roles over Vietnam, including this one operated by the 31st TFW from Tuy Hòa Air Base (AB) from 1968. (USAF via Museum of Aviation)

Left: F-105D Thunderchiefs are air-refueled en route to targets in North Vietnam. (USAF)

found its supersonic aircraft and nuclear-strike mission-trained crews were poorly suited to the tasks they were now required to perform.

What quickly proved more successful was the use of slow-moving aircraft that were able to carry large amounts of conventional ordnance and were able to loiter on task for long periods. Their effectiveness increased still further when they were able to work in close co-operation with ground forces. The fast-moving F-100s, F-4s and reconnaissance RF-101s struggled with the roles, especially having to make low-level attacks over often featureless terrain, frequently unable to visually identify targets they were expected to hit. They were particularly vulnerable to the large amounts of anti-aircraft artillery that the Vietnamese possessed. CAS techniques had to be re-learned, improved and expanded with aircraft such as the World War Two vintage A-1 Skyraider, which found a new role. As well as delivering air strikes, they often provided top cover to downed aircrews until combat search-and-rescue forces could reach them. However, the costs were high, with 150 Skyraiders lost on combat missions.

Forward Air Control (FAC) for air strikes was a vital and risky task with aircraft like the Cessna O-1 Bird Dogs, superseded by TAC-operated Cessna O-2A Skymasters and later more robust machines like the Rockwell OV-10 Bronco. Operating and combat losses in the FAC and psychological operations roles in which these aircraft were sometimes engaged to demoralize and confuse the enemy, were considerable – with 172 Bird Dogs, 104 O-2A Skymasters and 63 OV-10A Broncos lost up to 1973.

For attacks from above cloud or over featureless areas, F-105s had to be guided by better radar-equipped aircraft such as the B-66. (USAF)

The slow-moving A-1 Skyraider proved well suited to close air support (CAS) operations over Vietnam and for top-cover missions protecting downed airmen. (USAF)

The Cessna O-1 Bird Dog proved an excellent, if often vulnerable, forward air control (FAC) platform during the early phase of the Vietnam War. (USAF)

A contemporary shot of the unusually configured 'push-pull' Cessna O-2 Skymaster that proved a successful light FAC platform in Vietnam. (Kevin Wright)

TAC's airlifters also played a major role in South East Asia operations. From 1965, its C-130s began rotational basing assignments in South Vietnam, to supplement the five C-123 squadrons already there. As the war grew, some of TACs C-130 airlift units were transferred to the USAF's Pacific Air Forces, with new squadrons created in the continental US to address the increased demand for more aircrews. As well as South East Asia, TAC was expected to provide rotational aircraft for the European theatre and Pacific Air Forces' (PACAF) other commitments outside of Vietnam. Troop-carrier operations remained a TAC mission until December 1974, when its 14 squadrons of C-130s were transferred to Military Airlift Command (MAC).

Up until 1975, activated C-123K units were operationally gained by TAC and were widely used in Vietnam. (USAF/Sgt Rozalyn Dorsey)

In the approximately eight-year period up to 1973, total US combat and operational aircraft losses in South East Asia were staggering by today's standards. They included just over 1,250 USAF fixed-wing aircraft and helicopters, many from TAC-assigned units. Among the combat aircraft, approximately 382 F-105 D/F/Gs Thunderchiefs, 528 F-4 and RF-4C Phantoms, 243 F-100 Super Sabres, 39 RF-101 Voodoos, 61 CH/HH-3s and CH/HH-53s, 36 Air Force UH-1s, 56 B-57s, 22 A-37 Dragonfly and smaller numbers of other types including F-102s, F-104s and F-111As were lost. Among TAC's transport aircraft, losses were considerable too and included 19 C-7 Caribou, 21 C-47s, 53 C-123 Provider, 55 C-130 Hercules plus several AC-47, AC-119 and AC-130 gunships.

Following the immediate end of operations in South East Asia, the US military experienced a major downsizing from 1973, with the end of the draft and the transformation to an all-volunteer force. For TAC, in particular, those early post-Vietnam years were about reorientating the Command, consolidating units and rebuilding its preparedness and capabilities for wider operations. It was also a decade that saw a huge modernisation program with the introduction into service of major new combat types, the F-15, F-16, A-10 and the often less remembered A-7D Corsair II. These momentous changes radically improved TAC's combat capabilities through what would be the Cold War's deepest phase, followed by its sudden, unexpected conclusion.

Left: TAC gained the highly manoeuvrable C-7 Caribou, which had an outstanding short-field performance, and was ideal for South East Asia operations. (USAF/SSgt William Magel)

Below: The USAF procured 459 A-7D Corsair IIs as CAS aircraft, and they performed 12,928 missions in Vietnam. In the 1980s, most were passed to TAC-gained Air National Guard units. (USAF)

Chapter 3
Back to the Cold War

Early warning and air defense

The first of Boeing's E-3A Airborne Warning and Control Systems (AWACS) was delivered in 1977, and was a huge advance over its EC-121D 'Warning Star' predecessor that had been operating in the role since 1954. The E-3A harnessed major advances in electronics, with its distinctive rotating disc mounted above the fuselage, making it immediately identifiable. Advanced computing power and its pulse-Doppler radar technology made it an extremely capable platform, able to warn of approaching hostile aircraft and direct defending forces. TAC operated the entire USAF E-3 fleet, assigned to the 552nd Airborne Warning and Control Wing (AWCW) based at Tinker AFB in Oklahoma. It also provided crews for the US contribution to the 18 E-3As NATO purchased and based at Geilenkirchen in Germany. USAF E-3s were regularly deployed to several forward operating bases including Keflavik in Iceland, Elmendorf in Alaska and Kadena in Japan, plus short-term operations from other locations.

Having been briefly involved in the air defense of the continental United States from 1948 to 1950, TAC again assumed the role in 1979 when the decision was made to split up Air Defense Command (ADCOM). Its interceptor and ground radar elements became Air Defense, Tactical Air Command (ADTAC) and the other, mainly satellite early-warning related elements, passed to what later became Space Command. Within TAC, ADTAC had the same status as a numbered Air Force. During that period ADTAC began the replacement of its obsolete F-101 Voodoo and F-106A Delta Dart interceptors with F-15As and F-16As.

The EC-121D was used as a radar picket aircraft by the USAF, with the last retired in 1978. (NMUSAF)

Above: Operated by TAC, the Boeing E-3A Airborne Warning and Control System (AWACS) provided a quantum jump in airborne early warning (AEW) capability. (USAF/SSgt A Taninggo)

Left: The F-106A Delta Dart was a major element of US continental air defense forces when Air Defense Tactical Air Command (ADTAC) was formed in 1979. (USAF/SSgt Bill Thompson)

Two 107th Fighter Interceptor Squadron F-101 Voodoo interceptors, operated by ADTAC up to their final retirement in 1982. (USAF)

Alongside its F-106 Delta Darts, the 49th Flight Interceptor Squadron (FIS) at Griffiss AFB flew T-33As in the training role until 1986. (USAF/TSgt DG Plummer)

From the mid-1980s, the air defense F-101s and F106s were gradually replaced with more modern aircraft, including these F-15As of the 48th FIS. (USAF/Tsgt Lou Hernandez)

The move to TAC was regarded as an interim step, with the long-term goal being transferring the air defense mission from the active duty USAF to the Air National Guard. That process was not completed until 1990, as the Cold War slipped away and the task became a much lower priority.

For many years, the US military struggled to create a well-functioning and unified special operations capability, a goal finally achieved in 1987, with the formation of Special Operations Command. Before that, TAC units had long operated in special forces-related roles. In Korea, and later in South East Asia, its aircraft were used to infiltrate and extract agents and special forces personnel. In Vietnam, the combat search and recovery task became especially important for retrieving downed airmen, undertaking missions behind enemy lines and rescuing cut-off troops in remote regions. Early TAC special operations were mostly managed through the 4440th Combat Crew Training Group. Later, this was replaced by the 1st Air Commando Wing, and in 1974, the 1st Special Operations Wing at Hulburt Field in Florida. In 1982, the consolidation of Military Airlift Command's (MAC) specialized Air Rescue and Recovery Squadrons and TAC's special forces aircraft and crews began, as they were fully transferred to MAC's newly activated 23rd Air Force.

USAF Air Demonstration Squadron: Thunderbirds

The USAF's Air Demonstration Squadron, better known today as the "Thunderbirds," has traditionally been equipped with versions of TAC's frontline fighter types. From its beginning in 1953, this was the F-84G Thunderjet, until it was replaced by the F-100C Super Sabres in June 1956, and the team moved to Nellis AFB, Nevada. For the 1964 season, the team very briefly flew the F-105 until one example suffered a major structural failure resulting in the loss of the aircraft and its pilot. The team quickly moved over to fly the F-100D until the end of the 1968 season, when it was replaced by the F-4E Phantom. The team was assigned to the TAC under the control of the "USAF Tactical Fighter Weapons Center" on February 13, 1967. The Thunderbirds continued flying F-4Es up to 1974 when the squadron switched to the much smaller and fuel-economic T-38 Talon trainer, which better suited the economic straits of the post-Yom Kippur War oil crisis.

Above: The F-100 Super Sabre was used by the Thunderbirds Air Demonstration Squadron from 1956 to 1968. (Michael Benolkin)

Right: The F-105 Thunderchief was very briefly used by the team in the 1964 season, but a fatal crash revealed major airframe flaws that made it unsuitable for demanding aerobatic routines. (USAF)

The Thunderbirds have entertained crowds worldwide, with more than 3,000 displays performed before TAC's demise in 1992. Like all the world's major aerobatic teams, they have had accidents from time to time. The worst was the loss of four T-38s on January 18, 1982, in what became known as the Diamond Crash, when the four aircraft struck the ground together as they emerged too low from a loop. The team converted to the F-16A in 1983, upgrading to the F-16C in 1992.

When the oil crisis struck in 1974, the Thunderbirds moved away from their gas-guzzling F-4E Phantoms on to the much more economic Northrop T-38A. (USAF)

In 1983, the Thunderbirds converted to the F-16A, moving to the F-16C in 1992. (Kevin Wright)

Dual-basing

Following the removal of NATO-committed forces from France in 1966, after that country's withdrawal from the Alliance, the USAF designated TAC's 49th TFW at Holloman AFB in New Mexico as a 'dual-based' wing. This meant that although stationed in the continental US, they were always available for immediate 'return' to Europe as required. They practised this commitment every autumn by deploying F-4 squadrons to bases at Hahn and then Ramstein in Germany. Codenamed *Crested Cap*, the 49th TFW made regular deployments up to 1977 when they began conversion from the F-4D to the F-15A. From 1978, the 4th Tactical Fighter Wing at Seymour Johnson AB took over the commitment and made the annual deployments up to 1985, then on an irregular basis up to the end of the Cold War.

From 1966 to 1977, the 49th TFW at Holloman AFB, New Mexico, was "dual based" with that commitment tested by annual deployments to West Germany. (USAF)

The 4th TFW at Seymour Johnson AFB took over the dual basing from 1978 commitment from Holloman and made regular European deployments up to the end of the Cold War. (TSgt HH Deffner)

Chapter 4

The Creech Years

General Wilbur "Bill" Creech became TAC commander on May 1, 1978, and remained in post until November 1, 1984. He has been described as a "transformational" commander who introduced major changes. His focus was on warfighting and improving TAC's ability to do so at every level. He greatly improved its combat effectiveness through reforms to its training, by modernizing its equipment and vastly enhancing its preparedness. Perhaps the best testimony to his success came later in the way that TAC was ready to deploy and fight in the Gulf War of 1990–91, following the Iraqi invasion of Kuwait.

Drawing lessons from Vietnam, the first USAF "Aggressor" training units, utilized the highly agile F-5E Tiger II and Soviet-style tactics of the time. This adversary training became a key element of later large scale *Red Flag* exercises, with the first taking place in Nevada in December 1975. While it

Left: Gen Wilbur Creech was head of TAC from 1978 to 1984 and is regarded by many as a transformational commander. (USAF)

Below: The highly agile F-5E equipped TAC's "Aggressor" squadrons, the airframes being originally destined for the collapsed South Vietnamese Air Force. The aircraft could emulate the performance of Soviet fighter aircraft such as the MiG-21. (USAF/MSgt Paul Harrington)

The 64th and 65th Aggressor squadrons' F-5Es wore a variety of different paint schemes, some similar to those used on Soviet aircraft to make visual identification more challenging. (USAF)

greatly improved training realism for the aircrews, for Creech it was far from enough. When he assumed command of TAC in 1978, his first command conference outlined what he saw as the major shortfalls in its ability to successfully prosecute any future air war. He was determined to make aircrew training far more realistic and employ new technologies and training to enable more effective night operations. He recognized that not being able to mount effective offensive night-combat operations severely restricted the air forces' ability to engage an enemy. Creech became a firm proponent of advanced technology including targeting systems such as low-altitude navigation and targeting infrared for night (LANTIRN), secure communications such as HAVE QUICK radios and new precision-guided munitions.

Gen Creech was a firm proponent of advanced technology, including the low-altitude navigation-targeting infrared night (LANTIRN) pod being tested on this F-15C, which would enable TAC to operate effectively at night. (Paul Reynolds)

Red Flag, and the regular *Blue Flag* exercises that trained senior commanders in air operations, became an important avenue for Gen Creech to advance his more realistic training goal. He reformed the structure of the exercise so that it now more closely reflected what commanders believed the first two weeks of real air warfare would be like, rather than just repeating the first day of the air war several times over. So successful were they considered, that the scenarios grew in complexity, scale and number as more resources were invested in them. *Red Flag 1977* involved 55 aircraft; by 1984 that had swelled to 250; and later at times passed 400, with an ever-increasing emphasis placed on night operations. It also led to other developments, such as the introduction of *Green Flag* exercises in 1981, for growing specialist electronic warfare assets. Further spin-offs saw the introduction of *Copper Flag*, to more realistically test air defense capabilities. *Silver Flag* tested support functions including rapid runway repair, security forces and emergency medical support. *Black Flag* addressed rethinking wartime aircraft maintenance, with an emphasis on sortie generation.

At wing and squadron level, it was important to Creech for, "Each unit to become familiar with its wartime collocated operating bases" (ie, the airfields they would operate from during times of war). He wanted to ensure that his units became familiar with their areas of operations, "We should be able to deploy and hit the ground in a fighting posture and the only way we can accomplish this is by knowing everything possible about the deployment site." By October 1978, these ideas had evolved into the "Checkered Flag" concept, overhauling earlier contingency planning arrangements. While most of the effort was devoted to preparations for European operations, Korean and Middle East scenarios were regularly practised.

US and NATO war preparations relied on a massive, intricately choreographed airlift of forces to Europe prior to hostilities commencing. For TAC, this meant not just deploying its active duty units and crews but was also the gaining command for activated Air Force Reserve (AFRes) and Air National Guard (ANG) units. The arrangements were in constant flux, as aircraft fleets were modernized, assigned unit roles changed and readiness levels fluctuated. As *Checkered Flag* evolved, the number of practise deployments to Europe greatly increased. Creech was keen to ensure that units prepared their equipment

TAC aircraft were regularly deployed overseas. This F-111A from the 366th TFW at Mountain Home AFB, Idaho, is in formation with two South Korean F-4Ds in 1978. (Curt Eddings)

and trained their personnel for rapid deployment overseas. Those preparations were to be periodically tested by real unit deployments, usually for two-week periods but sometimes up to a month. Former NATO Supreme Commander Europe, US General Joseph Ralston, later explained that the changes in TAC were very noticeable between the time he had left to attend USAF Staff College in 1975 and his return to TAC in 1979. By then he said, "The quality of training was excellent… Everyone knew where they were going to be and we were much more combat-oriented."

Air Force Reserve units took part in overseas deployments too. F-105Ds of 507th TFG at Carswell AFB, Texas, visited RAF Sculthorpe in 1978. (USAF)

The F-4 Phantom comprized the greatest proportion of TAC combat power by the end of the Vietnam War. It was gradually replaced by the F-15 and F-16, as was the case for the 388th TFW at Hill AFB in 1980. (USAF/SMSgt Phil Lewis)

Chapter 5
COBs and Coronets

European deployments required the use of a vast number of airfields. It also necessitated TAC entering into bilateral 'host nation' base agreements with the governments of the UK, West Germany, Belgium, Netherlands, Italy, Denmark, Norway, Iceland, Greece and Turkey. These agreements defined each country's specific responsibilities, tasks and who would pay for them. The main issues were about individual airfield capacities, availability of adequate radio and communications facilities, suitable navigational aids, meteorological services, weapons and fuel storage, plus liquid oxygen supplies. From 1975 to 1992 there were approximately 250 TAC deployments to Europe, codenamed *Coronet*. Around 110 were from TAC active duty units and 140 from activated ANG and Air Force Reserve units that would be attributed to TAC in wartime. There were additional deployments for weapons competitions, in support of Air Defense Command on Keflavik, plus the annual 'Salty Bee' reconnaissance aircraft and the twice-yearly 'Crested Cap' visits by TAC dual-based units. In addition to the European deployments, there were many *Coronet* series deployment exercises held within the continental United States, Panama, Puerto Rico and the Pacific Air Forces area, including Japan and Hawaii. Working with US Central Command in the Middle East, TAC aircraft deployed to Egypt for regular *Bright Star* exercises during the 1980s and others such as *Proud Phantom*.

For *Salty Bee* 1982, RF-4Cs from the 363rd TRW at Shaw AFB, South Carolina, went to RAF Alconbury for a month-long deployment. (USAF)

US aircraft was regularly deployed to Egypt in the 1980s to train for war in the Middle East. During 1980, exercise *Proud Phantom* saw F-4Es of TAC's 347th TFW train with Egyptian F-4Es. (USAF)

For *Coronet Wrangler*, the 474th TFW deployed F-16s to RAF Bentwaters in 1982, its likely wartime operating base. During any war, RAF Bentwaters would have been largely empty as its resident A-10s forward deployed to West Germany to destroy Soviet armor. (USAF/TSgt Jose Lopez)

RAF Sculthorpe was a USAF standby base consisting of runways, hard stand taxiways, a few support buildings and some pre-positioned materials. It awaited the arrival of people and aircraft. (USAF/TSgt Jose Lopez)

At RAF Sculthorpe, in 1983, *Coronet Castle* saw all the base facilities temporarily reactivated for the deployment of a squadron of Ohio ANG A-7Ds. (USAF/TSgt Jose Lopez)

The types of bases that hosted TAC deployment were very varied, some being regular frontline airfields, others were just 'bare bones' fields, comprising of a runway and parking areas. Now declassified RAF and UK Ministry of Defence (MoD) records reveal how those plans evolved and were practised up to the end of the Cold War. In the UK, USAFE's HQ Third Air Force at RAF Mildenhall was responsible for its Main Operating Bases (MoBs) at Mildenhall, Lakenheath, Bentwaters/Woodbridge, Upper Heyford and Alconbury, which all housed major active-duty flying units. There were additional Stand-by Bases (SoBs) at Sculthorpe and Wethersfield. During any run-up to war, most MoBs were to be reinforced with additional aircraft and TAC units, sent from the US to the SoBs. However, these were insufficient, so TAC sought more airfields for contingency use. From 1974, the US and British governments earmarked specified RAF-operated airfields as Co-located Operating Bases (COBs), to host wartime US deployments.

Co-located operating bases

Airfields considered included the RAF Jaguar base at Coltishall and the Harrier base at Wittering. They were likely to be mostly empty during any wartime scenarios, as their resident aircraft were expected to be forward deployed to Norway, Denmark, Germany, Turkey or elsewhere.

Up to 1982, RAF Waddington would likely have been comparatively quiet, its resident nuclear-declared Vulcan squadrons dispersed to airfields across the UK and so their home airfield would have been operating well below capacity. RAF training bases such as Finningley and Leeming were also expected to be relatively quiet, with most flying training heavily curtailed or dispersed elsewhere. The final category of airfields considered included those owned by the UK Ministry of Defence, such as Boscombe Down and the Royal Aircraft Establishment (RAE) airfields at Bedford and Farnborough.

The Co-located Operating Base (COB) concept required the host nation to provide air traffic control and other support elements to allow TAC aircraft to use the host's airfields, such as at RAF Leeming for *Coronet Cactus* in 1982. (TSgt Jose Lopez)

In Britain, Coltishall, Fairford, Waddington and Wittering were in the first wave of identified COB bases, with the Technical Agreements and specific Joint Support Plans reached for each. In the planning period from 1977 to 1982, Wittering and Waddington were identified as A-7D Corsair II deployment bases, each for two 18-aircraft squadrons. Coltishall was expected to house up to two squadrons of 18 RF-4C Phantoms. HQ Third Air Force designated the existing USAF MoB units to 'parent' each COB location. Waddington was parented by the 20th TFW at Upper Heyford, Wittering, the 81st TFW at Bentwaters, and Coltishall, the 10th TRW at Alconbury. Soon Boscombe Down was earmarked for 48 F-111Ds and Finningley allocated two 18-strong F-4 Phantom squadrons. In common with many NATO airfields, a progressive Hardened Aircraft Shelter (HAS) construction program was planned for these bases, but they were only ever completed at Wittering and Boscombe Down. At each of the COBs, there were also proposals for extra weapons, fuel and liquid oxygen storage facilities.

Nine further locations were surveyed for a second wave of five more COBs. Soon, Leeming and RAE Farnborough were chosen to each host 24 F-4 Phantoms. RAF Odiham to provide the weapon storage facilities for Farnborough. RAE Bedford was earmarked to receive 48 F-4s.

By the 1980s, a large number of ANG squadrons were equipped with the A-7D Corsair II. These made frequent deployments to RAF Wittering and Waddington and occasionally the standby base at RAF Sculthorpe. At Waddington, after the wartime dispersal of the Vulcan force, it was planned that just eight aircraft would remain at their home base, so there would have been plenty of space to receive incoming US deployments. Details from the Waddington Joint Support Plan highlight some early ground support issues that had to be addressed, including a shortage of weapons' storage, the availability of adequate fire service cover and refuelling vehicles, as most were expected to have been sent with the Vulcans to their dispersal bases.

A TAC F-4E, deployed from Seymour Johnson AFB, banks away from the camera on a training flight over West Germany. (USAF)

Air National Guard deployments

Major deployments regularly tested the COB arrangements. Between July 9 and August 21, 1978, 18 A-7Ds from the TAC assigned 157th TFS South Carolina ANG, 166th TFS Ohio ANG and 146th TFS of the Pennsylvania ANG units arrived at Wittering for *Coronet Teal*. This was followed by later deployments including *Coronet Stallion* to RAF Waddington in 1979 with 15 Iowa and three South Dakota ANG A-7Ds. Some years later, *Coronet Buffalo* from May to June 1985 brought 24 Iowa ANG A-7Ds and 12 from South Dakota with more than 950 National Guardsmen to the Lincolnshire base. A final visit saw the Oklahoma ANG send 12 A-7Ds from the 138th TFG between June 3 and 15, 1991.

Right: A-7 Corsairs became regular visitors to the UK from 1978. On occasions, this included the rare two-seat A-7Ks, which is refueling from a KC-135. (USAF)

Below: A-7Ds from the 150th TFG, New Mexico Air National Guard (ANG) at RAF Wittering for *Coronet Canvas* in 1981. (USAF/Sgt Thomas Coaxum)

Although a Hardened Aircraft Shelter (HAS) area was constructed at RAF Wittering for deployed aircraft use, *Coronet Mail* in July 1983 saw the A-7s operate from this RAF airfield's main aircraft servicing platform. (USAF/Sgt Thomas Coaxum)

Part of the *Coronet Canvas* War Readiness Spares Kit (WRSK) in the hangar at RAF Wittering. (USAF/Sgt Thomas Coaxum)

MAC C-141s were vital for moving the equipment and personnel required for deployments. This 63rd MAW C-141B is landing at RAF Wittering for *Coronet Mail* **in July 1983. (USAF/SGT Thomas Coaxum)**

A-7D deployments to Wittering were usually smaller, but more frequent than those to Waddington. *Coronet Canvas* brought eight A-7s from the Oklahoma ANG in May and June 1981. Eighteen A-7D/Ks from the Pennsylvania and New Mexico ANGs from July 8 to 22, 1983 arrived for *Coronet Mail*. *Coronet Barracuda* saw 12 A-7D/Ks from the Oklahoma ANG return for two weeks in April 1985. *Coronet Gemini* brought 18 Corsairs from Pennsylvania and New Mexico in July 1987. The final two-week deployment was in June 1988, when *Coronet King* saw 12 more A-7s, again from the Oklahoma ANG.

To ensure the maintainability of its aircraft when operating overseas, TAC units relied on War Readiness Spares Kits (WRSK). These WRSKs were either pre-positioned at their intended wartime

On the ground, forklift trucks and K-loaders could be key to the speedy unloading of C-141 Starlifters bringing in the WRSKs. (USAF/SSgt Jose Lopez,)

deployment base or, more usually, airlifted in with them. Deployments typically involved between 160 and 320 personnel, dependent on the number and type of aircraft involved, accompanied by more than 100 tons of equipment and supplies in three to eight C-141 Starlifter flights.

Air National Guard F-4 Phantom deployments

Coronet Brave saw RAF Finningley receive 12 F-4Ds and 270 Guardsmen from the 170th TFS/183rd TFG, Illinois ANG, from June 12 to 25, 1982. Twelve 110th TFS Missouri ANG F-4Cs and 320 personnel visited nearby RAF Leeming, for *Coronet Cactus* from June 28 to July 9, 1982.

RAF Finningley was again the location for an F-4D Phantom deployment from June 3 to 17, 1983, when F-4Ds of the 121st TFS/113th TFW, Washington DC ANG, arrived for *Coronet Shield*. Major Rick Stallings piloted one of the 12 F-4Ds for that deployment. He had earned his wings with the District of Columbia (DC) ANG and had flown for more than eight years, first on the F-105D, then the F-4D before visiting the UK in 1983.

He explained: "We had several briefings beforehand and meetings with people that had been over before, so we felt pretty well prepared. The seven-and-a-half-hour non-stop Atlantic crossing from Andrews AFB felt incredibly long. It was rather uneventful; we hooked up with the tankers within half an hour of taking off and stayed with them all the way over. We refuelled six to eight times, constantly topping up just in case there were problems and we had to divert. One of our squadron commanders was onboard a tanker to monitor progress." This was the Wing's first major deployment for more than 30 years, supported by personnel flown in by MAC's C-141 transports.

"When we got to Finningley, there was a bit of weather so we did instrument approaches. I remember being exhausted, so we pretty much just had a meal and went to bed…RAF Finningley was absolutely great. It was a challenge for us all to operate in such a different environment. We flew missions around the

Coronet Brave **brought the 170th TFS of the Illinois ANG with 12 F-4Ds and 170 personnel to RAF Finningley in June 1982. (USAF/MSgt Don Sutherland)**

An F-4D taxies for departure from RAF Finningley during *Coronet Brave*. (USAF/MSgt Don Sutherland)

A TAC-gained 131st TFW Missouri ANG F-4C on the runway at RAF Leeming being released from the arrester cable after an emergency landing during *Coronet Cactus*. (USAF/SSgt Jose Lopez)

F-4Ds of the 113th TFW, DC ANG deployed to operate from European airfield locations on three occasions during the 1980s. (DF Brown)

UK and into Europe." The F-4Ds participated in Exercise *Central Enterprise* and for four days practised against targets in the Netherlands, Belgium and West Germany. In total, their F-4Ds flew more than 170 sorties in eight days. "I recall one mission to a Belgian bombing range, and on another, we did simulated airfield attacks in West Germany." Maj Stallings visited Europe twice more with the 113th TFW.

From April 19 to May 3, 1986, 12 Washington DC ANG F-4Ds operated from Keflavik in Iceland for *Coronet Kiowa*. Six aircraft briefly stayed at RAF Lossiemouth taking part in the RAF's *Elder Forest* air defense exercise, which included training with RAF Phantoms and making simulated attacks on the air defense radar station on Benbecula, in the Outer Hebrides. From September 10 to 24, 1988, 12 F-4Ds returned to Keflavik, supported by two KC-10A tankers for *Coronet Wizard*. Two of the Phantoms took on Keflavik's 24-hour quick reaction alert (QRA) alert commitment, ready to intercept any Soviet TU-95 Bears. Six other F-4Ds, 18 aircrew and 42 support staff made a three-day visit to Bardufoss AB in Norway from September 18 to 21. From there, the F-4Ds mounted simulated attacks against allied ships during NATO's *Teamwork '88* exercise, with the ships defended by US Navy and Norwegian fighters.

TAC F-111s and the UK

The UK was home to two long-range USAFE F-111 wings at RAF Lakenheath and RAF Upper Heyford. That made the UK a sensible basing location for deployed TAC F-111s too, given the type's generally more complex support requirements. The Ministry of Defence (MoD) airfield at Boscombe Down regularly received deployments, most close to a month-long, of active duty 27th TFW F-111Ds from Cannon AFB, New Mexico, operating from the specially constructed Hardened Aircraft Shelter areas. These included *Coronet Hammer*, involving 18 F-111Ds from May 7 to June 9, 1980; and *Coronet Archer* with eight F-111Ds in September 1983. From August 27 to September 24, 1986, *Coronet Comanche* involved 12 F-111Ds, accompanied by six EF-111As from the 366th TFW for *Coronet Papago*. *Coronet Diamond* involved 12 F-111Ds in June 1989.

F-111Ds from the 27th TFW at Cannon AFB, operated from a specially constructed shelter area during regular deployments to Boscombe Down airfield, including for *Coronet Comanche* in 1986. (Rob Schleiffert)

At the same time as the F-111Ds were at Boscombe Down in 1986, they were joined by six EF-111As of the 366th TFW for *Coronet Papago*. (Rob Schleiffert)

Poor serviceability and low mission readiness rates plagued the USAF throughout the 1970s. Creech used that first May 1980 *Coronet Hammer* deployment to demonstrate his assertion that this was more to do with spare parts availability rather than, as many in Congress and the US military asserted, the technical complexity of modern aircraft. In his 1982 Congressional testimony, Creech explained more about the *Coronet Hammer* deployment to Boscombe Down. "There they flew a full range of F-111 missions, at almost twice the required wartime rate, over only a 15-hour flying window daily, [because

The F-111Ds deployed to Boscombe Down required a huge amount of sophisticated avionics test equipment to be pre-positioned. (USAF/MSgt Tom Jacobus)

Hurry up and wait. 27th TFW personnel and their personal belongings await departure from Boscombe Down at the conclusion of *Coronet Hammer*. (USAF/TSgt John Marine)

Cannon's F-111Ds were involved in exercise *Team Spirit 1985*, which saw the 27th TFW deploy aircraft to South Korea. (USAF/MSgt David Craft)

of peacetime constraints] and once again, on a self-sufficient basis, operating out of its own WRSK. Moreover, this same F-111D squadron achieved an 86.4 percent Fully Mission Capable rate throughout the period of its deployment (contrasted with a 34 percent rate at its home station)." During their stay at Boscombe Down, they had required 1,361 spares items, of which all but 66 they had brought with them. Those few other items were sourced from other UK bases and support depots. "The sortie goals were exceeded and the unit flew well in excess of their wartime tasking." The F-111Ds had been scheduled to fly 505 sorties in the planned 20 flying days for *Coronet Hammer* but managed to fly 554. They had been "cross-serviced" at airfields in five different NATO countries and dropped ordnance at nine different ranges.'

Deployment support

The frequent TAC training deployments across the Atlantic required considerable use of European and US-based KC-135A and KC-10A tankers. They provided the multiple air refueling hook-ups the fighters required, supplemented by Military Airlift Command airlifting the necessary supplies and support staff.

Although the tankers were assigned to Strategic Air Command, a large proportion of their missions were in support of TAC, to meet their mobility requirements. From 1974, 128 KC-135As were gradually transferred to Air National Guard and Air Force Reserve units, to mainly help meet TACs growing air-refueling needs. For the KC-135s, this meant a great many "fighter drags" across the Atlantic. The introduction of the much larger and more capable KC-10A "Extender," brought significant change to transatlantic crossings. Lt Col (Ret'd) Jon Mickley was already highly experienced on KC-135s both as an active duty serviceman and reservist and was one of the first KC-10 pilots. He explained: "My KC-10A time was wonderful. Being involved from such an early stage gave us the opportunity to write the book on the KC-10A. Not so much the flying the airplane, but the tactics and procedures used.

Above: The KC-135s and KC-10A tankers, belonging to Strategic Air Command (SAC), were vital to any rapid and effective TAC deployment. (USAF/SSgt Keith Reed III)

Below and opposite: The cavernous interior of the KC-10A offered huge flexibility. For deployments, it could be readily adapted to carry a mix of passengers and freight while also refueling 'chicks' on the way to their destination. (USAF/Sra Gordon Bell)

The KC-10A was unlike any other airplane in the Air Force. The magic thing about it was we could be air refuelled ourselves. The airplane hauls vast amounts of fuel great distances; can carry up to 75 people and 17 cargo pallets."

These capabilities brought, "A major change in the procedures used for 'fighter drags' across the Atlantic. Before we used a fleet of KC-135s to refuel groups of fighters off the US East Coast." Others would then fly out to meet them as they approached Europe, maintaining racetrack patterns for hours, waiting to refuel them. "We persuaded the Air Force to send KC-135s out to refuel our KC-10As off the US East Coast rather than the fighters. They flew a shorter mission and did one big offload to us and went home while we accompanied the fighters across the water. That saved many KC-135 flight hours spent flying on station."

"In April 1985, we accompanied 18 RF-4Cs from Bergstrom AFB, Texas, to Aviano AB in Italy. Four KC-10As departed Barksdale AFB, Louisianna, with personnel and cargo for the deployment, each with a group of RF-4s 'chicks

'Fighter drags' refueling aircraft crossing the Atlantic or Pacific became much easier with the KC-10A compared to the KC-135As that carried far less fuel. (USAF)

In April 1985, four KC-10As moved 18 RF-4Cs of the 67th TRW, together with associated personnel and equipment, directly from Bergstrom AFB, Texas, to Aviano AB in Italy. (USAF/CMSgt Don Sutherland)

in tow'. Off the US East Coast, we took on fuel from KC-135As. We crossed with the RF-4Cs and topped them-up six times going over. KC-135As came out from Mildenhall and fuelled us, as receivers, over the eastern Atlantic for the balance of the 9.5 hour flight on to Italy. This dual role, refuelling and cargo, became our 'bread and butter' activity."

The frequent Atlantic crossings of all these TAC *Coronet* deployments saw the Command utilize its own airborne command and control assets, to assist its smooth operation. These assets consisted of two (a third had crashed in 1977) immaculately maintained "Head Dancer"-configured EC-135Ks, operated by the 8th Tactical Deployment Control Squadron at Tinker AFB. They were equipped with multiple VHF, UHF, HF radios (including secure sets), teletype equipment and later had a SATCOM capability. The airborne "Mission Control Team" was approximately 11 people, usually headed by a TAC colonel. They monitored en route weather, flight progress and regularly passed situation reports back to HQ TAC at Langley. The EC-135Ks were comfortably equipped, with aircraft serial 53-3118 described as having thick carpeting, nine bunks, a fully equipped galley, airline seats, tables and high-quality soundproofing.

TAC used its "Head Dancer"-configured EC-135K command post to monitor the progress of its major aircraft deployments (Rob Schleiffert)

Chapter 6

TAC Looks to the Middle East

The US Rapid Deployment Force (RDF) was created in 1979, to enable operations outside Europe and Korea, mainly with an eye to any potential Middle East crises. TAC became an integral part of the Force, it's Ninth Air Force commander was responsible for the RDF's USAF element. The increased US commitment to Egypt following the Camp David Accords, saw a series of joint US-Egyptian exercises begin, codenamed *Bright Star*, with the first held in 1980. By 1983, the RDF had evolved to become US Central Command (CENTCOM), and the scale and number of exercise participants grew. The RDF and CENTCOM's air commander were able to call on all the major combat units assigned to TAC. CENTCOM grew in importance during the 1980s and came to prominence with the Iraqi invasion of Kuwait in August 1990.

Following Saddam Hussein's invasion, the United States immediately ordered a massive mobilization of its armed forces for deployment to the region. TAC assets were a major component of CENTCOM's combat power and represented the largest proportion of USAF aircraft sent to the region. While the years of war preparations were never tested for real in Europe, the experience gained from them was vital to what became Operations *Desert Shield* and *Desert Storm*. James Kitfield explained in 1990 that, "General Horner and his airmen benefited from the years of realistic training and logistics planning that preceded the Gulf War …[he must have] said a silent prayer of thanks to all the Checkered Flags,

A 363rd TFW F-16 with a Jordanian F-5F. The formation of Central Command saw TAC units regularly deploy to the Middle East for training with friendly air forces. (USAF/TSgt Bob Simons)

Blue Flags and operational-readiness inspections that Bill Creech had force-fed Tactical Air Command, getting them in the habit of deploying quickly as a way of life."

Preparations in the region had begun a decade before, when in March and April 1980, General Creech and his senior TAC staff visited several countries in Europe and the Middle East. He recognized the need to establish relationships and create a logistics infrastructure within the Gulf region and received permission from defense minister, Prince Sultan bin Abdul Aziz, to pre-position munitions and equipment in Saudi Arabia. In their meeting, Creech outlined the need for bare bases, with just runways, fuel access, and potable water. He also suggested the Saudis 'overbuild' some of their own main operating bases, so that US forces could operate from them if they requested US assistance. General Larry Welch, one of Creech's deputies, later recalled that "the assumption was that if they would build it, we would come when needed. They did and we did."

By the summer of 1990, Tactical Air Command consisted of three numbered Air Forces with six Air Divisions (ADs), a direct reporting Air Division and three special tactical, training and test establishments that all reported directly to HQ TAC. First Air Force was headquartered at Langley AFB, alongside HQ TAC, and was responsible for supporting North American Aerospace Defense Command (NORAD). It was mostly comprized of ground-based assets, as the interceptor alert aircraft, maintained by NORAD, were now largely drawn from Air National Guard units. Organisationally, TAC's 24th Air Division was responsible for the eastern half of the United States and the 25th Air Division covered the western half. Air assets were centred around just 50 F-15Cs, of which half covered the air defense of Iceland with the 57th Fighter Interceptor Squadron (FIS), at Keflavik AB, and the remainder with the 48th FIS at

The Tactical Air Weapons Defense Centre was responsible for testing and developing new air defense equipment for the USAF. (Cindy Farmer)

Langley. Alongside other TAC units at Tyndall AFB in Florida was the 325th Tactical Training Wing, which undertook F-15 fighter crew training and was home to TAC's Air Defense Weapons Centre. It was responsible for developing tactics and evaluating new air defense-related equipment items, and operated airframes converted to QF-100D and QF-106A pilotless target drones, for live-fire missile practice.

Weapons Meet

The USAF World Wide Weapons Meet, a competition intended for air defense units, unofficially known as "William Tell," began in June 1954, with Tyndall AFB, Florida, becoming its home from 1958. TAC participated for the first time in 1976, and three years later, assumed sponsorship for the weapons meet, following the creation of ADTAC. Its first sponsored meet in 1980, included ten teams, from active duty USAF and ANG, F-4, F-101 and F-106 units and a Canadian Forces CF-101 team. In 1982, Tactical Air Command officially changed the name of the meet to the USAF Air-to-Air Weapons Meet. It also saw Pacific Air Forces and USAFE join the competition, with the first appearance of the F-15.

Teams gathered at Tyndall to fly different mission profiles against manned aircraft and some live fire missions against Full Scale Aerial Targets (FSATs), such as the QF-100 unmanned drone conversions. The drones were operated from Tyndall, by the then 82nd Tactical Aerial Target Squadron using civilian contractor staff. During live fire missions, far from all the target drones were destroyed, with surviving aircraft returned to Tyndall, for further use. Onboard self-destruct systems could be used to destroy any damaged, but still airborne target, or they could be brought down by one of Tyndall's resident escorting chase fighters. There were separate contests for the unit weapon controllers, maintenance personnel and weapons loaders.

During *William Tell '84*, technicians in a mobile control van guide the take-off of a QF-100 Super Sabre drone. (USAF/TSgt Edward Boyce)

A line-up of QF-100 drones at Tyndall AFB. (USAF/SSgt Russ Pollanen)

The launch of a Firebee target drone during *William Tell '82*. (USAF/TSgt Frank Garzelnick)

Above: Two QF-100D target drones, complete with Soviet stars, being prepared for their next mission at *William Tell '88*. (USAF/SSgt Charles Taylor)

Left: QF-100 operator Dick McKibben guides his drone over the air weapons range during *William Tell '86*. (USAF/SSgt Dave Mcleod)

A QF-100D in flight. The drones were rarely completely destroyed during the *William Tell* weapons meets. (USAF/TSgt Guido Locati)

Prior to the F-100 drone conversions, PQM-102A Delta Daggers were used, such as this one during *William Tell '80*. (USAF)

Chapter 7

TAC Goes to War in the Gulf

HQ Ninth Air Force was located at Shaw AFB in South Carolina and parented ten tactical wings, with approximately 750 aircraft. Most were tasked to operate in support of US Central Command in the Middle East but could be deployed for operations anywhere in the world, if required. By 1990, this included the 1st TFW with three squadrons of F-15C/Ds at Langley AFB and the similarly sized 33rd TFW at Eglin AFB in Florida. The 4th TFW at Seymour Johnson AFB in North Carolina, with three squadrons, had recently transitioned to the multi-role F-15E, having relinquished its old F-4Es. F-16s were in abundance, with three squadron-strength Wings at Moody AFB, Georgia (347th TFW), and Shaw AFB (363rd TFW), and a two-squadron wing at Homestead AFB, Florida (31st TFW). The 23rd TFW at England AFB, Louisiana, and the 354th TFW at Myrtle Beach, South Carolina, each flew three squadrons of A-10As. The 507th Tactical Air Control Wing at Shaw AFB, parented the 21st Tactical Air Support Squadron, with its Forward Air Control OV-10A Broncos that were gradually being phased out of service. MacDill AFB, also in Florida, was home to the 56th Tactical Training Wing, with four F-16 squadrons, dedicated to crew training.

Three squadrons of F-15Cs from the 1st TFW at Langley AFB were among TACs highest readiness units. (USAF)

A 33rd TFW F-15C Eagle from Eglin AFB, Florida, armed with AIM-9 Sidewinder and AIM-120 AMRAAM missiles, passes along the Florida coast. (USAF/TSgt Kit Thompson)

TAC's 4th TFW had a dual-based commitment that was later extended beyond Europe, to potentially become worldwide as part of the USAF's Rapid Deployment Force. (USAF/TSgt HH Deffner)

The 4th TFWs transition to the F-15E, began in late 1988 was complete in July 1991, spanning the Gulf War. (USAF)

The 347th TFW arrived at Moody AFB, Georgia, in 1975 from Korat Royal Thai AFB in Thailand to fly F-4Es up to 1988. (USAF/TSgt Frank Garzelnick)

In 1990, the 347th TFW flew three squadrons of F-16As from Moody AFB. (Mike Kopack)

The 363rd TFW's F-16s regularly visited Europe, including for *Coronet Gauntlet* at Rygge AB in Norway, in August 1983. (USAF/SSgt Ernest Sealing)

From 1985, the 31st TFW operated F-16s at Homestead AFB, Florida, and briefly wore the "ZF" tail codes carried on its old F-4Es. (USAF/Sra Marvin Krause)

By 1987, the 31st TFW's F-16s had changed their tail codes to the more usual style "HS." (USAF/TSgt Lee Schading)

A 23rd TFW A-7D Corsair II banks over a training range close to Nellis AFB, in 1980. By 1990 the wing flew A-10As. (USAF/TSgt Frank Garzelnick)

Passing through Sigonella AB in Italy after the end of the Gulf War, this 23rd TFW A-10A is armed with AIM-9 self-defense Sidewinder missiles. (USN/PHAN Cinelli)

Tactical Air Command 1946–92: Cold War Air Power

During Exercise *Thunderhog V* in 1983, a 354th TFW A-10 Thunderbolt II taxies out from its Myrtle Beach base. (USAF/SSgt Phil Schmitten)

A 20th Tactical Air Support Squadron OV-10A Bronco banks during a flight out of Shaw AFB, South Carolina, in 1990. (USAF/TSgt HH Deffner)

The four squadrons of the 56th Tactical Training Wing (TTW) that operated from MacDill AFB, Florida, was one of two wings that handled the massive pilot-training requirement for its F-16 force. (USAF)

At Bergstrom AFB in Texas, the 12th Air Force was much more diversely equipped. It was numerically the largest of TAC's three Air Forces, with more than 1,000 aircraft under its control. They were shared between five subordinate Air Divisions and 13 flying wings. A substantial number of those aircraft were assigned to the F-16-equipped 58th Tactical Training Wing (TTW) and 405th TTW flying F-15A/Es at Luke AFB, Arizona, of the 832nd Air Division. At Holloman in New Mexico were the four squadrons of the AT-38B equipped 479th TTW.

Twelfth Air Force combat power was concentrated in the remaining Air Divisions. The 35th TFW with its F-4E and Wild Weasel F-4Gs at George AFB in California (831st AD), and F-15A/B flying 49th TFW at Holloman (833rd AD). The 836th AD was by far the largest, it was responsible for the three-squadron A-10A formal training unit, the 355th TTW at Davis-Monthan AFB. The airfield was also home for the three-squadron 602nd Tactical Air Control Wing's OA-10As – with one squadron at George AFB. Flying activities at Bergstrom AFB comprized the 67th Tactical Reconnaissance Wing, with two operational and two training squadrons of RF-4Cs. Two operational squadrons and a training unit of F-111Ds of the 27th TFW were at Cannon AFB, New Mexico. The 366th TFW at Mountain Home AB possessed an operational and a training squadron of F-111As plus a specialist EF-111A squadron. The 388th TFW at Hill AFB in Utah, operated three squadrons of F-16C/Ds. Most exotic of all was the 37th TFW from Tonopah, deep in the Nevada desert, with its three squadrons of F-117As.

Two 58th TTW F-16s, an F-15 and an F-5 Tiger II from the 405th Tactical Training Wing, all based Luke AFB, Arizona, in 1979. (USAF/TSgt Bob Simons)

Five 58th TTW F-16s in tight echelon over Arizona. (USAF/TSgt Bob Simons)

F-15As from the 405th TTW over the massive ramp space at their home, Luke AFB, Arizona. (USAF/TSgt Bob Simons)

A 479th Tactical Training Wing AT-38B from Holloman AFB, used as part of the Lead-In Fighter Training (LIFT) program for pilots. (USAF/TSgt Jose Lopez)

The 37th TFW's "Wild Weasel" F-4Gs flew the dangerous air defense suppression mission, intended to take out enemy anti-aircraft sites. (USAF/SSgt Joe Smith)

Two F-15s from the 49th TFW at Holloman. The Wing became purely an air defense unit after completing conversion from the F-4E to the F-15A in 1978. (USAF)

An A-10A Thunderbolt II from the 355th Tactical Training Wing at Davis Monthan AFB, was the type's formal training unit. This A-10A is armed with an AGM-65 Maverick missile and is working over the Gila Bend Tactical Range. (USAF/SSgt Bob Simons)

The forward air control OV-10As of the 27th Tactical Air Support Squadron (TASS) were part of the 602nd Tactical Air Control Wing, operated from George AFB, California, with the wing headquartered at Davis-Monthan. (USAF/TSgt Jose Lopez)

The 23rd TASS at Davis-Monthan AFB was the first squadron to convert from the OA-37 Dragonfly to the OA-10A in 1987. (USAF/TSgt Michael Haggerty)

At Bergstrom AFB, Texas, one of the 67th TRW's training units was the 45th Tactical Reconnaissance Training Squadron as the special markings on this RF-4C celebrate. (USAF/CMSgt Don Sutherland)

The low-level flying Cannon AFB F-111Ds of the 27th TFW were regular participants at TAC's *Red Flag* exercises. (Ken Hackman)

Banking over the Nellis AFB range, an F-111 of the 391st Tactical Fighter Training Squadron, 366th Tactical Fighter Wing, is carrying a full load of Mark 82 low-drag bombs. (Ken Hackman)

The 366th TFW EF-111As were a high-demand, high-value asset, seen here at Howard AFB in Panama in 1988. (USAF/SSgt Matthew Gildow)

A 388th TFW F-16A at Hill AFB, Utah, temporarily operating out of Holloman AFB during Exercise *Border Star '81*. (USAF)

F-117As of the 37th TFW at Langley AFB on their way to the Gulf in 1990. (MSgt Boyd Belcher)

Down at Howard AFB in Panama was the 830th Air Division, home to the 24th Composite Wing, with its OA-37Bs, often engaged in training activities with South American air forces. In August 1977, the 474th TFW was activated at Nellis AFB and equipped with three squadrons of F-4Ds passed to them from the 48th TFW at RAF Lakenheath in England. The 474th TFW received its first F-16As in November 1980, which it operated until September 1989 when its aircraft were passed to Air National Guard units and the wing deactivated.

As well as the assigned Air Forces, HQ TAC controlled several major direct reporting units. These included the 28th Air Division's, 552nd Airborne Warning and Control Wing. It was responsible for the USAF's E-3B/C AWACS airborne early warning force at Tinker AFB in Oklahoma. It maintained three additional squadrons in Iceland; Elmendorf, Alaska; and Kadena in Okinawa, that managed the temporarily deployed aircraft. Also at Tinker AFB were the EC-135Ks of the Eighth TDCS. At Keesler AB in Missouri, the secretive EC-130Es of the Seventh Airborne Command and Control Squadron operated in the airborne battlefield command and control role, guiding tactical and close air support operations. Finally, TAC had control of the awesome EC-130H "Compass Call" communications jamming aircraft, stationed at Davis-Monthan AFB, which would play a key role in the Gulf War.

TAC also parented the USAF Tactical Fighter Weapons Center at Nellis AFB and the USAF Tactical Air Warfare Center at Eglin AFB. Both establishments operated a wide range of frontline types including A-10s, F-15s, F-16s, F-111s, T-38s and RF-4Cs. At Nellis, the 57th Fighter Weapons Wing's emphasis was on developing combat tactics – closely related to the *Red Flag* program, under the control of the 4440th Tactical Fighter Training Group. The Fighter Weapons Center also parented the USAF Air Demonstration Squadron, the Thunderbirds, which had been flying F-16s since 1983. Eglin AFB was the main location for operational testing of new USAF weapons under the USAF Tactical Air Warfare Center. This was managed via its four Tactical Test Squadrons and Groups using either their own aircraft or those loaned for specific programs.

An OA-37B Dragonfly from the 24th Composite Wing at Howard AFB, Panama. The unit often trained partner air forces in South America. (USAF/MSgt Herbert Cintron)

The 24th Composite Wing was one of the last USAF operators of the Cessna O-2A, photographed at San-Pedro Sula AB, Honduras, in 1985. (USAF/SSgt Kendrick Thomas)

In formation over the Grand Canyon are F-16As of the 474th TFW. The wing regularly deployed aircraft to Europe in the late 1980s. (USAF/SSgt Wayne Evans)

The 552nd Airborne Warning and Control Wing at Tinker AFB maintained squadrons in Iceland, Alaska and Japan to operate forward-deployed aircraft. (USAF/TSgt Olivo Reynaldo)

Above: Elusive EC-130E Hercules of the 7th Airborne Command and Control Squadron at Keesler AFB used as an Airborne Battlefield Command and Control Centre to support air operations in theatre. (USAF/Sra Tana Hamilton)

Left: TSgt Ken Clover, onboard an EC-130E, sets the frequency position on a communication monitor during Exercise *Team Spirit '86* over South Korea. (USAF/TSgt Danny Perez)

In an unusually public situation, an EC-130E, at Addis Ababa airport, in 1989, works in support of a search and rescue (SAR) mission. (USAF/MSgt Bill Thompson)

A superlative jamming platform, a "Compass Call" EC-130H takes off from Germany in 1989. (USAF/MSgt Dave Casey)

One of TAC's direct reporting units was the 57th Fighter Weapons Wing (FWW) at Nellis AFB, which operated a wide range of aircraft, including A-10s, F-15s, F-111s and F-16s. (Ken Hackman)

An F-15, from the 57th FWW, was used to develop and improve Air Force tactics and operational doctrine. (USAF)

In 1987, the Tactical Air Warfare Center at Eglin AFB undertook the "Hill Project" testing the grey-on-grey camouflage used on the F-16 to evaluate its effectiveness for Wild Weasel F-4Gs. (USAF/TSgt Bob Marshall)

An RF-4C loaned to the Tactical Air Warfare Center, at Eglin, for test purposes (USAF)

UH-1Ns were operated by TAC's 4460th Helicopter Squadron at Indian Springs Auxiliary Airfield as one of its direct reporting test units. This image was taken much later, but it still wears the same paint scheme as it did in 1990, but now with the added "ET" tail code. (USAF/Samuel King)

By 1990, TAC had reached the zenith, equipped with modern, highly capable aircraft and weapons systems and was well-practised in rapid overseas deployments. It was a capability that was soon fully tested in the harsh operating environment of the Middle East.

TAC in the desert

TAC's activities in the Gulf during 1990 and 1991, a mission it had long prepared for, would turn out to be the Command's last major operation, as plans were already being made in Washington DC that would result in its demise. On August 2, 1990, Iraqi forces invaded Kuwait. Rapidly overrunning the tiny state, they provoked a massive, immediate response from the United States. Operation *Desert Shield*, the rapid deployment of air forces to the region, was intended to deter any possible roll-on of Saddam Hussein's forces into Saudi Arabia. In quick succession, came air defense F-15s followed by dual role F-15Es and F-16s, A-10s and a squadron of F-117As with supporting E-3 AWACS aircraft, electronic warfare and reconnaissance elements.

To deploy and operate in the region for *Desert Shield* and *Desert Storm*, TAC was reliant on SAC's tanker force and the C-5s, C-141s and C-130s of Military Airlift Command. This was the first major operational test for the KC-10A force, with their contribution out of proportion to their numbers. Involved from the start of the US response on August 7 and 8, 1990, they refueled 48 fully armed F-15Cs from the 1st TFW at Langley AFB heading to Saudi Arabia.

Retired Col Victor Herrera, who later accumulated more than 4,000 hours as a KC-10A pilot and squadron commander, had joined the USAF in 1984. He flew KC-135As for two years before he joined the KC-10A squadron at Barksdale AFB. He explained, "At the start of *Desert Shield* we were called in very early and told we were leaving Barksdale, loaded with our maintainers and equipment to keep us operating. We air-refuelled from KC-135s over the East Coast and rendezvoused with the Langley F-15s. Halfway across the Atlantic we refuelled the fighters, took on more gas ourselves over the eastern Atlantic and then on into the Mediterranean. We topped them up again and headed on to Saudi Arabia, an over-16-hour flight. Within 12 hours of arrival at King Abdul Aziz International Airport we were refuelling them on CAP missions. We had quickly brought personnel, supplies and a wing of F-15s to Saudi Arabia all in one fell swoop. For the first three weeks, we were constantly refuelling F-15s and E-3 AWACS, expecting Saddam to invade Saudi Arabia at any moment."

E-3 Sentry aircraft deployed to Saudi Arabia at the start of Operation *Desert Shield* to provide early warning of any hostile Iraqi air activity. (USAF/CMSgt Don Sutherland)

On August 10, 1990, the first 4th TFW F-15Es, then transitioning from the F-4E, arrived at Al Khark AB, Saudi Arabia. (USN/PHAN Chad Vann)

F-117s were rapidly deployed to King Khalid AB where there were Hardened Aircraft Shelters available to protect them. (USAF/TSgt HH Deffner)

The F-117As landed at Langley AFB, their first stopover on the long transit flight to Saudi Arabia for *Desert Shield*. (USAF/MSgt Belcher)

Forty-eight F-15s from the 1st TFW crossed non-stop from Langley AFB to Dhahran in Saudi Arabia in two waves over two days, arriving fully armed and ready to fly combat air patrols. (USAF)

For the duration of *Desert Shield*, several KC-10As operated from Morón AB, Spain. (USAF/SSgt Louis Briscese)

The KC-10A's ability to carry much bigger loads than the KC-135 eased the large-scale early rapid deployments of units to Saudi Arabia. (USAF)

TAC aircraft and unit deployments for *Desert Shield/Storm*

Date	Type	No.	Unit/ Home Base	Location
Aug 08, 90	F-15C	24	71 TFS/1 TFW, Langley AFB	Dhahran
Aug 08, 90	E-3B/C	5	552 AW & CW, Tinker AFB	Riyadh
Aug 09, 90	F-15C	24	27 TFS/1 TFW, Langley AFB	Dhahran
Aug 10, 90	F-15E	24	336 TFS/4 TFW, Seymour Johnson AFB	Al Khari AB
Aug 10, 90	F-16C	24	17 TFS/363 TFW, Shaw AFB	Al Dhafra
Aug 11, 90	F-16C	24	33 TFS/363 TFW, Shaw AFB	Al Dhafra
Aug 17, 90	F-4G	24	561 TFS/35 TFW, George AFB	Shaikh Isa
Aug 18, 90	A-10A	24	353 TFS/354 TFW, Myrtle Beach AFB	King Fahd Intl
Aug 20, 90	A-10A	24	356 TFS/354 TFW, Myrtle Beach AFB	King Fahd Intl
Aug 21, 90	F-117A	18	37 TFW, Tonopah TR	King Khalid AB
Aug 25, 90	RF-4C	6	106 TRS/117 TRW, Birmingham IAP, Alabama ANG (August–December)	Shaikh Isa AB
Aug 26, 90	EC-130H	2	41 ECS/28AD, Davis-Monthan AB	Bateen AB
Aug 29, 90	F-15C	10	58 TFS/33 TFW, Eglin AFB	Tabuk AB
Aug 30, 90	F-16C	24	4 TFS/388 TFW, Hill AFB	Al Minhad
Aug 30, 90	EC-130H	3	41 ECS/28AD, Davis-Monthan AB	Bateen AB
Aug 31, 90	A-10A	24	74 TFS/23 TFW, England AFB	King Fahd Intl
Aug 31, 90	F-15C	12	58 TFS/33 TFW, Eglin AFB	Tabuk AB
Aug 31, 90	E-3B/C	1	552 AW & CW, Tinker AFB	Riyadh AB
Sep 01, 90	F-16C	24	421 TFS/388 TFW, Hill AFB	Al Minhad
Sep 02, 90	F-15C	2	58 TFS/33 TFW, Eglin AFB	Tabuk AB
Sep 02, 90	A-10A	24	76 TFS/23 TFW, England AFB	King Fahd Intl
Sep 15, 90	EF-111A	14	390 ECS/366 TFW, Mountain Home AFB	Taif AB
Dec 01, 90	OA-10A	6	23 TASS/602 TACW, Davis-Monthan	King Fahd Intl
Dec 04, 90	F-117A	18	37 TFW, Tonopah TR	King Khalid AB
Dec 20, 90	E-3B/C	1	552 AW & CW, Tinker AFB	Riyadh AB
Dec 29, 90	RF-4C	4	192 TFS/152 TRG, Reno IAP, Nevada ANG	Shaikh Isa AB
Dec 29, 90	F-15E	23	335 TFS/4 TFW, Seymour Johnson AFB	Al Kharj AB

Date	Type	No.	Unit/ Home Base	Location
Dec 30, 90	F-16A	24	157 TFS/169 TFG, McEntire ANGB, South Carolina ANG	Al Kharj AB
Jan 02, 91	E-3B/C	1	552 AW & CW, Tinker AFB	Riyadh AB
Jan 03, 91	F-16A	18	138 TFS/174 TFW, Hancock Field, New York ANG	Al Kharj AB
Jan 06, 91	OA-10A	6	23 TASS/602 TACW, Davis-Monthan	King Fahd Intl
Jan 06, 91	A-10A	18	706 TFS/926 TFG, NAS New Orleans, Louisiana ANG	King Fahd Intl
Jan 08, 91	F-16C	24	69 TFS/347 TFW, Moody AFB	Al Minhad
Jan 10, 91	E-3B/C	2	552 AW & CW, Tinker AFB	Riyadh AB
Jan 12, 91	RF-4C	12	12 TRS/67 TRW, Bergstrom AB	Shaikh Isa AB
Jan 17, 91	E-3B/C	2	552 AW & CW, Tinker AFB	Incirlik AB

Source: USAF (Gulf War Air Power Survey)

In January 1991, F-16As from the 174th TFW of the New York ANG deployed to Al Kharj AB for *Desert Storm*. (USAF/MSgt John Luszcz)

F-16As from the 169th TFG, South Carolina ANG at McEntire NGB, deployed to Al Kharj AB on December 30, 1990. (USAF)

An RF-4C Phantom of the 117th TRW, Alabama ANG. Reconnaissance assets were in short supply, but USAF commanders were cautious about fielding the ageing RF-4Cs. (USAF/Sgt Wright)

During December 1990 and January 1991, preparations for what became *Desert Storm* gained momentum. Many more squadrons of offensive airpower continued to arrive in theatre, including more F-117As, F-15Es, F-16s and A-10s that included a few activated Air National Guard flying units. The war began on January 17, led by precision missile strikes, by US Army AH-64 Apache helicopters, SAC B-52s and TAC F-117A attacks on high-value targets, followed by the rest of the coalition's massive assembly of air forces. TAC EF-111As and Compass Call EC-130Hs, provided electronic suppression with F-4G Wild Weasels striking active enemy radars. That first wave of coalition attacks aimed at destroying Iraq's air defense radar, missile sites and airfields with a full range of missiles and precision munitions. Over subsequent nights, systematic attacks continued on the Iraqi air defense network and quickly extended to search and destroy Scud missile sites, which could have brought Israel into the war.

Four RF-4Cs from the 152nd Tactical Reconnaissance Group (TRG) of the Nevada ANG deployed to Shaikh Isa AB (where all the RF-4Cs were concentrated) on December 29, 1990. (USAF/Spc Joe Moore)

EF-111A 'Raven' electronic warfare aircraft, such as this example from the 366th TFW were vital protection for coalition high-speed, low-level, deep penetration attacks. (USAF/TSgt Rose Reynolds)

In December 1990, another 18 F-117As arrived at King Khalid AB, their temporary Saudi home. (USAF/SSgt HH Deffner)

Four F-4G Wild Weasels from the 37th TFW carry various weapons including AGM-88 high-speed anti-radiation missiles, AGM-45 Shrike, AGM-65A Maverick missiles and CBU-58 cluster bombs, for hitting enemy air defense sites. (Fred Jones)

Entering service in late 1982 with the 41st Electronic Combat Squadron (ECS) at Davis-Monthan AFB, the EC-130H *Compass Call* proved itself in Gulf operations in 1990–91. (USAF/SSgt Fernando Serna)

EC-130H Compass Call

By the mid-1980s, the EC-130H Compass Call had become the USAF's modern "single-purpose jamming platform" with a very advanced electronics suite. *Desert Storm* was its first major operational test. Five EC-130Hs from TAC's 41st Electronic Combat Squadron (ECS) at Davis-Monthan were deployed to Bateen, in the United Arab Emirates, at the end of August 1990. Crews usually consisted of 13 people – a flight crew of pilot (aircraft commander), co-pilot, navigator and flight engineer. The nine "back end" crew, were supplied by the Electronic Security Command mission. Led by the Mission Crew Commander (an electronic warfare officer) were a: high band operator (HBO), acquisition officer (a cryptologic linguist), four analyst operators (linguists), a signals analyst/operator and an airborne maintenance technician.

Operating well away from the frontline, they were protected by "Barrier CAP" fighters, as were other high-value assets, that flew high above them to defend against possible Iraqi interceptor attack. Flying at operational altitudes, never officially confirmed, believed to be between 20,000ft and 28,000ft, the EC-130s long-duration missions could be extended by air refueling. Their early missions saw them employed in the passive intelligence collection role, listening in on Iraqi radio and electronic transmissions. But while the Compass Call aircraft were effective intelligence gatherers, their purpose was to gather actionable intelligence that could be used to disrupt enemy communication links. During operations, enemy transmissions could be automatically jammed, using a predetermined threat list, or examined by the on-board linguists and analysts, who selected individual frequencies to jam. In wartime, its highest priority was to target the communication components of enemy's integrated air defense networks. These included Iraqi surface-to-air

The 13-strong rear crew in the EC-130H included linguists and operators able to jam and spoof enemy communications. (USAF/SSgt Fernando Serna)

(SAM) systems, Ground Controlled Intercept sites, plus the communication links between them all. Meanwhile, the EF-111As and US Navy EA-6Bs provided temporary jamming along the routes being used by allied attack aircraft to hit enemy targets, Compass Call also worked in conjunction with the 35 TFWs Wild Weasel F-4Gs in their suppression of enemy air defenses (SEAD) role.

Compass Call's capabilities were described as battle-changing, largely predicated on an old electronic warfare aphorism: "if you can't talk you can't fight." So powerful were their jamming capabilities that they were sometimes called upon to demonstrate them during large training exercises – but only for short periods. They would soon be asked to "Knock it off," because their jamming was so effective that other exercise participants were unable to accomplish anything. The EC-130H crews had more selective options available too. These included using their onboard linguists to successfully spoof enemy communications, making it necessary for them to resort to time-consuming authentication procedures.

Compass Call missions effectively denied the Iraqi Air Force and military commanders the ability to use their VHF, UHF and other communication links. Where no alternative landline communications existed, they totally isolated frontline Iraqi units from their higher commanders and headquarters. The missions proved particularly important in the first hours of the 1991 air offensive as Allied forces began neutralizing Iraq's integrated air defenses. During the campaign, Compass Call operators flooded the Iraqi frequencies with noise, sometimes using heavy metal music, which earned some missions the radio station nickname 'KJAM'. Iraqi anti-aircraft artillery quickly adopted the habit of simply firing their guns skyward, in 30-minute-long barrages, when they detected widespread frequency jamming, suspecting that an air attack was imminent. Compass Call missions were then occasionally employed as deception missions, jamming the Iraqi's frequencies, to provoke pointless anti-aircraft barrages.

The Compass Call electronic warfare capabilities were very powerful and able to selectively jam individual frequencies, or complete bands, at the same time. (USAF/SSgt HH Deffner)

As the air war successfully progressed, preparations for the ground offensive intensified. Iraqi ground defenses, armor and troop concentrations bore the brunt of strikes from SAC B-52s, as coalition ground attack aircraft prepared the battlefield. That final phase of the War famously lasted just 100 hours from February 24 to 28. In the time leading up to the ground war, large numbers of A-10s, worked with US Army attack helicopters. They cleared Iraqi armor and ground positions ahead of the routes through which allied ground forces were due to advance.

During that 100 hours, the A-10s came into their own, flying CAS for US and coalition troops. As allied forces advanced, the Iraqi retreat soon turned into a rout. As their armored and motorized forces tried to escape Kuwait, A-10s were at the forefront of destroying them. Warthog pilots, Capt Eric Salmonson and Lt John "Karl" Marks completed more than seven hours in the air and destroyed a record 23 vehicles on February 25, 1991. They headed towards a Republican Guard tank position, identified by the squadron overnight, 80 miles inside Iraq. Lt Marks said, "The night guys had done what we normally do, attacked

A-10As were used to clear ground routes ahead of coalition armored advances. (USAF/TSgt Rose Reynolds)

A 354th TFW A-10A Thunderbolt II from Myrtle Beach AFB. During *Desert Storm*, most operations were flown at medium altitudes to reduce the possibility of damage or loss. (USAF/TSgt HH Deffner)

the leader and trailer so that they were bottled up." Working with an OA-10 Forward Air Controller and two more A-10s from Myrtle Beach, they divided the area between them. "We were in and had tanks burning within five minutes." In their first mission, they destroyed eight Iraqi vehicles, with a combination of Mavericks and the A10's highly effective GAU-8 cannon, then returned to the FOL for refuelling and re-arming. Expecting to go back on to 30-minute ground alert, "We got out, walked into the Squadron and immediately they said 'the Marines want you'."

"We had words, and hopped in our jets and were airborne 20 minutes later." The pair killed eight more vehicles and on a third and final mission destroyed another seven.

Chapter 8
From TAC to Air Combat Command

As with all the other major USAF Commands, the end of the Cold War saw their demise, or perhaps more accurately, transformation. TAC's great strength of being able to rapidly deploy massive amounts of airpower across the world was amply demonstrated by the just-ended *Desert Storm* operation. It had only been possible because of the decades of preparation to deploy to Europe, to respond to an expected massive attack on Europe by the Soviet Union. The implosion of the USSR had brought a major change to the US military's strategic environment. Expectations were now that future conflicts were likely to be comparatively small-scale, such as the dissolution of Yugoslavia, then unfolding.

Retrenchment was the immediate issue, reducing the number of bases, aircraft and personnel that could no longer be justified following the Soviet collapse. A second element, heavily backed by then USAF Chief of Staff General Merrill McPeak, was the concept of "Composite Wings," given traction by Gulf War success. There, multiple types of USAF and allied aircraft had operated alongside each other, often fulfilling very different roles. The example often cited was the aircraft used in Operation *Proven Force*, against northern Iraq from Incirlik Air Base in Turkey during *Desert Storm*. There, senior commanders had very effectively exploited the different strengths of the many varied aircraft types placed under their control to maximum effect.

A third major component of the transformation would see the proposed new command effectively absorb Strategic Air Command, with its bomber, tanker and missile forces. It would acquire 18 SAC bases and became responsible for all USAF nuclear forces, although these were transferred to Air Force Space Command the following year.

Flying units transferred to Air Combat Command on June 1, 1992

Base	Major Unit	Primary Aircraft Types
Barksdale AFB, LA	2nd Wg	B-52G, KC-135A (ex SAC)
Beale AFB, CA	9th Wg	KC-135Q, U-2R (ex SAC)
Bergstrom AFB, TX	67th RW	RF-4Clex TAC
Cannon AFB, NM	27th FW	F-111D/E/F/G (ex TAC)
Carswell AFB, TX	7th Wg	KC-135A, B-52H (ex SAC)
Castle AFB, CA	93rd Wg	B-52G, KC-135A/R (ex SAC)
Davis-Monthan AFB, AZ	355th FW	A-10A, OA-10A (ex TAC)
Dyess AFB, TX	96th Wg	B-1B, KC-135A (ex SAC)
	463rd AW	C-130H (ex MAC)
Eaker AFB, AR	97th Wg	B-52G, KC-135A (ex SAC)

Base	Major Unit	Primary Aircraft Types
Ellsworth AFB, SD	28th Wg	B-1B, KC-135R, EC-135A/C/G/L (ex SAC)
	44th SMW	LGM-30F (ex SAC)
England AFB, LA	23rd FW	A-10A (ex TAC)
Fairchild AFB, WA	92nd Wg	B-52H, KC-135R (ex SAC)
Francis E. Warren AFB, WY	90th SMW	LGM-30G/118A (ex SAC)
George AFB, CA	35th FW	F-4E/G (ex TAC)
Grand Forks AFB, ND	319th Wg	B-1B, KC-135R (ex SAC)
	321st SMW	LGM-30G (ex SAC)
Griffiss AFB, NY	416 Wg	B-52G, KC-135R (ex SAC)
Holloman AFB, NM	49th FW	F-15A/B to F-117A (ex TAC)
Homestead AFB, FL	31 FW	F-16C/D (ex TAC)
K.I. Sawyer AFB, MI	410th Wg	B-52H, KC-135A (ex SAC)
Langley AFB, VA	1st FW	F-15C/D (ex TAC)
Loring AFB, ME	42nd Wg	B-52G, KC-135R (ex SAC)
Luke AFB, AZ	58th FW	F-15E, F-16C/D (ex TAC)
MacDill AFB, FL	56th FW	F-16C/D (ex TAC)
McConnell AFB, KS	384th Wg	B-1B, KC-135R (ex SAC)
Minot AFB, ND	5th Wg	B-52H, KC-135A (ex SAC)
	91st SMW	LGM-30G (ex SAC)
Moody AFB, GA	347th FW	F-16C/D (ex TAC)
Mountain Home, ID	366th Wg	F-111A, EF-111A (ex TAC)
Myrtle Beach AFB, SC	354th FW	A-10A (ex TAC)
Nellis AFB, NV	57th FW	A-10A, F-15C/D/E, F-16C/D (ex TAC)
Offutt AFB, NE	55th Wg	EC-135C, RC-135U/N/W (ex SAC)
Pope AFB, NC	317th AW	C-130E (ex MAC) became 23rd Wing in June 1992
Seymour Johnson AFB, NC	4th Wg	KC-10A, F-15E (ex TAC)
Shaw AFB, SC	363rd FW	A-10A, OA-10A (ex TAC)
Tyndall AFB, FL	325th FW	F-15A/B (ex TAC)
Whiteman AFB, MO	351st SMW	LGM-30F (ex SAC)
Wurtsmith AFB, MI	379th Wg	B-52G, KC-135A (ex SAC)

Source: *World Air Power Journal*, Fall 1992

Composite Wings

The Composite Wing concept, first experimented with by TAC in the 1950s, re-emerged in the late 1980s. Now sometimes referred to as "an air force in a box," it was much the same idea. USAF Chief of Staff Gen Merill McPeaks vision saw some wings being equipped with a mix of aircraft types. They were to train together so that when deployed for operations they were already a well-integrated package and could commence operations immediately, requiring minimal external support. It was envisioned as part of the post-Cold War expectation that future wars would largely be small in scale. The plan was heavy on manpower, training and maintenance requirements as individual wings could operate up to five aircraft types, which made it very expensive. The idea was gradually abandoned in the early 2000s mainly because of its relative cost.

The first Composite Wing to form was the 4th Wing at Seymour Johnson AFB in 1991, with a mix of F-15Es and KC-10As. It lasted just four years. However, perhaps the 366th Wing at Mountain Home AFB was the best-known of these "super wings." Originally, it consisted of squadrons equipped with F-15Cs, F-15Es, F-16Cs, KC-135Rs, and B-52s (in 1996 were swapped for B-1Bs). The idea was abandoned by 2007 when all the other aircraft types had moved elsewhere apart from the F-15E Strike Eagles.

A KC-135R, F-15s and an F-16 from the 366th Wing, Mountain Home AFB, Idaho, fly over the pyramids, Egypt. (USAF/TSgt Dave Nolan)

An F-15C, from the 366th Wing at Mountain Home AFB, taxies into position at Cario West airfield in Egypt. (USAF/Sra Steve M Martin)

A 4th Wing KC-10A Extender, from Seymour Johnson AFB, drops back after completing an in-flight refuelling from another KC-10A during a training flight. (USAF/TSgt HH Deffner)

Change and continuity

Air Combat Command (ACC) was formally activated on June 1, 1992, assuming control of all fighter resources based in the continental United States, all bombers, reconnaissance platforms, battle management resources, and intercontinental ballistic missiles (ICBMs) too. Furthermore, ACC had some tankers and C-130s allocated for use by its composite wings.

ACC's first decade was a turbulent one, marked by frequent organisational changes and transfers of responsibility, much as had happened during its early history. For example, its Combat Search and Rescue (CSAR) mission was transferred to Air Mobility Command in February 1993. Also in 1993, control of the USAF's ICBM force was transferred to Air Force Space Command (AFSPC), where it stayed until 2009 when it was transferred to the newly created Air Force Global Strike Command (AFGSC). F-15 and F-16 flying training was moved over to Air Education and Training Command (AETC) in July of the same year. In the other direction, most of Air Mobility Command's C-130s, except those from the 23rd Wing, plus those permanently assigned to USAF's European and Pacific Air Forces, were transferred across to ACC. All the KC-10A and KC-135 tankers, except those KC-135Rs at Mountain Home AFB, as part of the 366th Wing and KC-10As from the 4th Wing at Seymour-Johnson AFB, went to AMC. TAC's C-130s passed back to AMC in April 1997. The CSAR mission transferred to Air Force Special Operations Command (AFSOC) in October 2003, only to return to ACC in April 2006.

While the Command's name changed in 1992, the roles and tasks of today's ACC essentially remain those of TAC, as it evolved during the Cold War. Through the experiences of Korea, Vietnam, Cold War Europe and the 1991 Gulf War, TAC became skilled at successfully deploying its aircraft and manpower to any part of the world and ready to engage in combat operations – a worthy heritage passed to its successor.

Other books you might like:

FINLAND'S AIR FORCES — FROM NEUTRAL TO NATO — KEVIN WRIGHT
Air Forces Series, Vol. 6

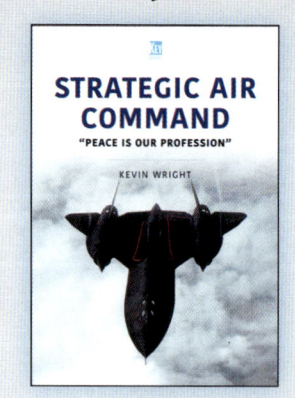

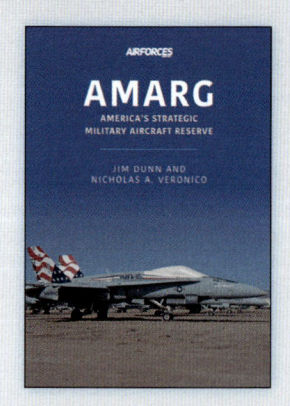

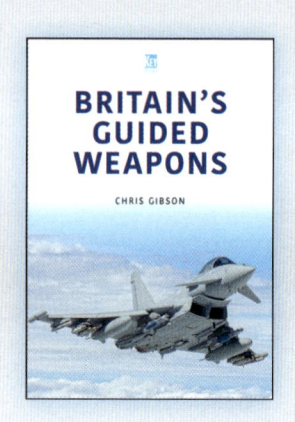

STRATEGIC AIR COMMAND — "PEACE IS OUR PROFESSION" — KEVIN WRIGHT

AMARG — AMERICA'S STRATEGIC MILITARY AIRCRAFT RESERVE — JIM DUNN AND NICHOLAS A. VERONICO

HIGH DESERT DEPLOYMENT — NAVY COLOR ON DISPLAY AT NAS FALLON — JIM DUNN & NICHOLAS A. VERONICO

BRITAIN'S GUIDED WEAPONS — CHRIS GIBSON

MARINE AIR-GROUND TASK FORCE — The Pinnacle of Combined Arms Warfare — SCOTT CUONG TRAN & NICK TRAN

For our full range of titles please visit:
shop.keypublishing.com/books

VIP Book Club

Sign up today and receive
TWO FREE E-BOOKS

Be the first to find out about our forthcoming book releases and receive exclusive offers.

Register now at **keypublishing.com/vip-book-club**

Our VIP Book Club is a 100% spam-free zone, and we will never share your email with anyone else. You can read our full privacy policy at: privacy.keypublishing.com